IMAGES
of America

QUONSET POINT
NAVAL AIR STATION
VOLUME II

Quoset and Comfair Quonset's air squadrons, carrier air groups, fleet air wings, and aircraft carriers, plus the products of the great industrial naval air station's A&R/O&R/NARF (Naval Air Rework Facility) plant served oceans, seas, and continents worldwide. For 34 years locations included the Artic, the Antarctic, Ireland, Great Britain, Norway, Italy, Greece, Sweden, Turkey, the Azores, Portugal, North Africa, France, Israel, Lebanon, Iceland, Newfoundland, Greenland, Labrador, Cuba, San Diego (CA), Hawaii, Midway Island, Wake Island, the Philippines, the Carolines, the Marshalls, Tarawa, Tinian, Saipan, Guam, Okinawa, New Zealand, Australia, Japan, China, French Indochina, Argentina, Thailand, Korea, and Vietnam. Here, a pimple-faced Civil Air Patrol Cadet (CAPC) student pilot strikes a *Sierra Hotel* pose in front of a Grumman Cougar jet trainer as a disgusted Fleet Air Detachment line crew looks on. Quonset's Visiting Plane Ramp hosted a wonderful variety of aircraft for more than 33 years. The aircraft is an F9F-8T buno 147328, BE-17, Marine Fleet Training Squadron One (VMT-1) up from MCAS Cherry Point on Armed Forces Day, May 1961. (Paul Tierney/Semper Fi/Author)

IMAGES
of America

QUONSET POINT
NAVAL AIR STATION
VOLUME II

Sean Paul Milligan

ARCADIA
PUBLISHING

Published by Arcadia Publishing
Charleston, South Carolina

Library of Congress Catalog Card Number: Applied For

For all general information contact Arcadia Publishing at:
Telephone 843-853-2070
Fax 843-853-0044
E-mail sales@arcadiapublishing.com
For customer service and orders:
Toll-Free 1-888-313-2665

Visit us on the internet at www.arcadiapublishing.com

*Dedicated to My Beloved Family
and the unsung Heroes of Naval Aviation:
the Enlisted Men of the United States Navy,
Marine Corps, and Coast Guard.*

(Drawing by Kate Huntington)

CONTENTS

ACKNOWLEDGMENTS

My deepest gratitude is extended to my two mentors, Mr. William T. Larkins and Captain Zip Rausa, USN (RET), for their all-weather, unrelenting help and faith in my work; to Jane Jackson, Curator of the Phillips Memorial Library; to Bob Lawson, photographer and longtime ramrod of *The Hook*; to all hands at the Quonset Air Museum; and to all the other organizations and individuals who contributed their efforts. I especially want to thank Staff Sergeant William J. "Bill" Curry, Rhode Island Air National Guard, for his sharp eyes and unwavering dedication to the *spirit* of United States Naval Aviation. Lastly, I wish to thank the United States Marine Corps for taking me in. Semper Fi, brothers, Semper Fi.

INTRODUCTION

Our Navy first gave the aeroplane serious attention more than five years before the Wright flyer first smelled the sky at Kittyhawk. On March 25, 1898, the assistant secretary of the Navy, Theodore Roosevelt, recommended that two officers "of scientific attainments and practical ability" examine Professor Samuel P. Langley's flying machine and report upon its practicability and its potential for use in war.

War did come 19 years later, and more than 570 naval aircraft and 18,000 officers and men were sent overseas to sink the Hun in the air, on the ground, under the ground, on the sea, and under the sea.

As early as 1918, the General Board for Naval Affairs recommended that a seaplane base be established on Narragansett Bay, Rhode Island, either at Newport or Quonset Point to protect the Northeast from German submarine and surface raider attack. Had the war continued into 1919, a seaplane base, capable of operating more than three dozen large long-range flying boats would have been constructed at Quonset.

Despite the absence of war after the signing of the Armistice on November 11, 1918, Navy interest in employing the Narragansett Bay area for flight operations continued. By 1920, a hangar and ramp were constructed on Gould Island to handle seaplanes and kite balloons that were to be employed by the Newport Naval Torpedo Station (NTS) in aerial torpedo and torpedo plane development. On August 30, 1921, two torpedo planes, PT-1's built by the Naval Aircraft Factory in Philadelphia, were assigned to the small East Passage Island, and by late December, they were installed in what would become the Navy's oldest contiguous flying organization, the NTS Air Detail. Thus was spawned the naval aviation heritage of Narragansett Bay.

As has been recounted in *Quonset Point, Volume I*, President Roosevelt created a "Neutrality Patrol" to protect all shipping operating in America's eastern sea frontier after Germany invaded Poland in September 1939. It is believed that the first "Neutrality Patrol" in FDR's Navy was launched from Newport in the NTS PBY-3 Catalina flying boat. Four months later, ground was broken for a giant Northeastern seaplane base with accommodations for no fewer than three squadrons of large patrol flying boats. A few months later, what was planned to be a seaplane base was greatly expanded to a full-fledged industrial naval air station that could simultaneously berth and service *four* aircraft carriers and had runways capable of operating the largest and heaviest land planes known or planned. The station also provided state-of-the-art industrial and scientific development facilities that overhauled thousands of combat aircraft and developed sonar, magnetic, radio, radar, and other equipment used to detect the enemy in the air as well as on and under the sea, measurably helping the Navy sail through the German and Japanese forces. Known as "the Pensacola of the north," NAS Quonset Point and her Command Echelon, Commander, Fleet Air Quonset (ComFair Quonset), formed, reformed, trained, and equipped two enormous Fleet Air Wings plus many "jeep carrier" composite squadrons that helped sweep the Nazi U-boat menace from the Atlantic, while more than half of her 45 air groups rode the fast carriers across the Pacific to the land of the Kamikaze and hard-fought Victory, Sweet Victory. It is here that the story of the skill, Yankee work ethic, drive, devotion to duty, and sacrifice of the Quonset family, Navy and civilian, continues.

Credit Legend

MIT = Massachusetts Institute of Technology Museum
NA = National Archives
NHC = Naval Historical Center
PC = Providence College—Phillips Memorial Library
QAM = Quonset Air Museum
RAF = Royal Air Force
RCN = Royal Canadian Navy
USMC = United States Marine Corps Semper Fi
USN = United States Navy
USNI = United States Naval Institute
USCG = United States Coast Guard
USAF = United States Air Force

One

VICTORY!

Victory, Sweet Victory! Cheerful Marines greet the first plane to land on Guam, a Grumman TBF-1C Avenger torpedo bomber, after it was recovered from the Japanese on July 20, 1944. By this time, a large portion of Pacific Fleet carrier aviation had Quonset origins. A year later, half of the Carrier Air Groups that participated in victory flights over Tokyo Bay on the day of the Japanese surrender, V-J Day, had been formed or reformed at Quonset Point. (USMC/Curry)

The first Nazi U-Boats destroyed by any United States force were dispatched by Quonset originated Patrol Squadron Eighty-Two (VP-82) starting on March 1, 1942, when a squadron PBO-1 Hudson sank the U-656 west of Newfoundland. VP-82, the Navy's first land plane patrol squadron, was established at Quonset two weeks after the Japanese sneak attack on Pearl Harbor. (USN/Irish)

Quonset's Project SAIL developed Magnetic Anomaly Detection (MAD) gear, which, coupled with retro rockets and the efforts of Quonset's unique Anti-Submarine Development Squadron (ASDEVRONLANT), contributed greatly toward victory in the Battle of the Atlantic. This PBY-5A Catalina from Quonset's Fleet Air Wing Seven, equipped with special ASW camo, radar, MAD, and retro rockets, was on the hunt and ready to fire. (USN/Fairwing Seven)

Quonset trained and supported many of the "jeep carrier" ASW escort Composite Squadrons that maintained the ocean bridge to England, which insured success in Europe and V-E Day. Land, sea, and carrier-based aircraft operating under or originating from Quonset's command echelon, Commander, Fleet Air Quonset (ComFair Quonset), were responsible for half of all the Nazi submarines sunk by U.S. Naval Aviation in the North Atlantic Theater during World War II. This F4F-4 29-GF-4 Grumman Wildcat was from Escort Fighter Squadron Twenty-Nine. (USN)

Top-secret airborne APS radar and CIC systems developed by Quonset's night combat Project AFIRM, sub-killing ASDEVRONLANT, and Project CADILLAC and the Navy/MIT Mickey "Spraycliff Observatory" at Beavertail Point, Jamestown, measurably helped win the Battle of the Atlantic and beat the Japanese Kamikaze in the Pacific. Pictured here is an Project AFIRM Twin Beech AT-7C (SNB-2C) Navigator with AN/APS-6 radar. (MIT Museum)

One of the very first Neutrality Patrol flights in "FDR's Navy" originated in Newport at NAF Gould Island during early September 1939, with the NTS Air Detail's PBY-3 Catalina. Formerly with Cape May's VJ-4, this Air Detail PBY-3 (ex 4-J-7) on Quonset's Seaplane Ramp in 1941 may have been the one that flew the first Neutrality Patrol. Quonset began inshore patrols with VS-2D1 in January 1941, and followed that with long-range off-shore patrols by VP-52 in March. (USN/PC)

A variety of aircraft flew off-shore ASW patrols and convoy escort with Quonset's Fleet Air Wings (Fairwing Seven and Nine), including Martin PBM Mariner flying boats and Consolidated PB4Y-1 four-motor land lanes. The majority of the work, however, was done by the ubiquitous PBY (pictured above) and the Lockheed PV-1 Ventura. Shown here is a PV-1 over Narragansett Bay, VB-125 (ex-VP-82) from Quonset's Fairwing Nine on July 24, 1943. This squadron destroyed *four* U-boats and put several others out of the war. (USN/FAW-9/Irish)

Comfair Quonset established 27 Fast Carrier Bombing Squadrons and equipped them first with old but faithful and quite capable Douglas Dauntless dive bombers . . . (*Marine Corps Gazette*)

. . . and then later, with the tricky but big, powerful, and heavily armed Curtiss SB2C Helldivers. (USN/USNI)

Comfair Quonset established 61 torpedo bomber squadrons. Torpedo Four (VT-4) was established aboard the USS *Ranger* on January 10, 1942, with six Douglas TBD-1 Devastators. Old "Rowboat" had minimum hangar space and the flying coffins took up a lot of room normally occupied by fixed wing SBD scouts and bombers. VT-4 was soon re-equipped with TBFs. Torpedo One Fifty-Four (VT-154) was established at Quonset with Convair TBY-2 Sea Wolves during June 1945. The other lucky 59 all got the highly successful TBF/TBM Avengers. (USN/NA)

Comfair Quonset established 42 Fast Carrier Fighting Squadrons VF, 11 Escort Carrier Fighting Squadrons VGF/VC, 20 Fast Carrier Fighter Bomber Squadrons VBF, plus more than 12 Fast Carrier Night Fighting Squadrons VF(N) plus detachments. Many were equipped with F4F/FM Wildcats or F4U/FG/F3A Corsairs, but most fought the war, day and night, in the cockpits of the backbone of the flat top Navy—the Grumman F6F Hellcat. This F6F-5 Hellcat, believed to be from Quonset's own Fighting Sixteen, is pictured here launching for a strike against Japan from the USS *Randolph* (CV-15) a few weeks before V-J Day. VF-16 was the first Fighting Squadron born at Quonset back in 1942. (USN/NA)

14

NAS Quonset Point and Comfair trained 60 carrier air groups of every class, including CVG, CVG(N), CVLG, CVLG(N), CVEG, and VC. More than half saw heavy combat before the end of the war. The tough and savvy training provided by NAS Quonset and Comfair didn't come cheap. This fighter crashed into a live ammo bunker along Runway 1/19 during the summer of 1943. (USN/NA)

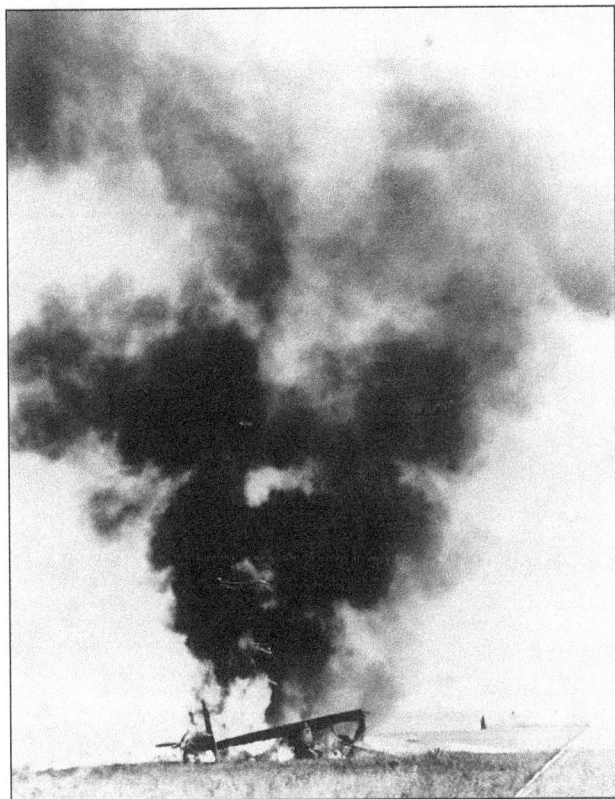

Combat operations from Quonset during the Battle of the Atlantic were also tough. This patrol plane burned after crashing on the air station infield during the spring of 1942. (RAF/53 Squadron)

No fewer than *ten* ComFair Quonset-established Fast Carrier Air Groups gave the Japanese homeland its final wartime blows on August 15, 1945. They were as follows (in order): CVG-94, CVG-16, CVLG-47, CVLG-27, CVG-85, CVG-86, CVG-88, CVG(N)-91, CVLG-50, and CVG-83. All of the Fast Heavy Carrier Air Groups (CVG) carried a full compliment Fighter-Bomber Squadrons (VBFs), a concept totally originated and developed by Comfair Quonset. The road to victory for all of them started right here. (USN/Lawson)

No orders to (or worse yet, back to!) the foreboding, Kamikaze-filled Pacific skies for these Quonset flying sailors. Amen. (Quonset A&T/Podnar)

Two

PEACETIME

After victory came peace. The very first V-J Day was celebrated right after Japan's surrender with a huge open house that was the first ever hosted by the great naval air station. Such was the urgency of total war. Dozens of static displays, including this one, were placed between the Crash House and Land Plane Hangar One (LPH-1). Shown here are an ASW gray TBM-3E "M 2" from Quonset's NAF Martha's Vineyard, an all-blue TEEB "H 2" from Quonset's NAF Hyannis, a diminutive FM-2 ASW gray Composite Squadron (VC) Eastern Wildcat, and a *million* dark blue Grumman F6F-5 Hellcats all adorned with "K" for "Quonset" on their tails. (USN/PC)

Wholesale demobilization of America's military began immediately after V-J Day under the Harry Truman administration, prompting the more than 5,000 civilians working at Quonset's enormous Assembly and Repair plant (A&R) to rightly fear for their jobs. There was still plenty of peacetime work to do, though, so many jobs were saved as A&R moth-balled thousands of wartime flying machines, including many at nearby NAS South Weymouth. (USN/PC)

Honoring the wartime contributions of Quonset's civilian workforce, mostly Rhode Islanders, the Navy went all out to save Quonset A&R from the Truman-inspired chop list. Seven major industrial naval air stations were on this list and Quonset was near the top. The officer in charge (OinC) of A&R, a Navy commander, personally went to Washington and saved the day. Quonset was back in the fleet overhaul business again as scores of PV-1 and PV-2 patrol planes, as well as similar R50 cargo and staff transports, reported in for the full "Quonset means Quality" treatment. This photo was taken at Quonset's Acceptance and Transfer Unit ramp with the Admiral's barge, a Lockheed R50-5 Lodestar, in 1946. (Quonset A&T/Podnar)

The real manna from Heaven that A&R's OinC brought home to Rhode Island was Project ROGER, which saw more than 200 R4D (Navy and Marine DC-3s) transports fully overhauled and modified for all manner of work. Most received airliner-class accommodations and amenities while others became School Ships (R4D-7 navigator trainers, see Volume I), or were fitted out for radar countermeasures (ECM), luxury VIP transport, cold weather operations or, as seen here, ASW training and development. R4D-5S buno 17173 7L-173, assigned to NAS Los Alamitos, May 12, 1963, came to Quonset A&R from San Diego in November 1946. (USN/Curry)

This C-47J (R4D-6) buno 50753 DA-753 of Marine Corps Headquarters and Maintenance Squadron Thirty-Two (H&MS-32) MCAS of Beaufort, South Carolina, c. 1972, was inducted into A&R from San Diego during April 1946. She first went to Navy VR-1 in 1947. (USMC/Beaufort)

During 1946 and early 1947, Quonset prepared six R4D-5s and two J2F Grumman Duck amphibians for Admiral Byrd's expedition to the Antarctic as part of Project HIGHJUMP. Duck worked from the survey ship USS *Tanner* (AGS-15) and the ice breaker USS *Edisto* (AGB-2), while ski-equipped R4D-5Ls launched with JATO from the Quonset carrier USS *Philippine Sea* (CV-47) on January 29, 1947, and flew 600 miles to Little America. RADM Richard E. Byrd rode in the first ship off. When not on the ice, the Ducks were cared for by Quonset's Utility Squadron, VU-5. HIGHJUMP Goonie peaks its nose through Duck wings at Quonset A&R in the fall of 1946. (USN/PC)

A&R also cared for some of Naval Aviation's oddities. A piston-and-jet powered Curtiss XF15C-1 compound fighter was tended to at A&R before the Navy retired it. The Navy passed on this one while it waited for a real jet fighter, which it got in the form of the McDonnell FD-1/FH-1 Phantom. In pure jet FH-1s, Quonset's VF-17A became America's first real carrier based jet squadron after carquals off Block Island aboard the USS *Saipan* (CVL-48) on May 5, 1948 (see Volume I). The Quonset Air Museum (QAM), located at the former great naval air station, is the proud owner of this handsome, historic machine, buno 01215. (Larkins)

Quonset's flying sailors were a long way from the "Jet Age" when this Scout Bomber Second Class Curtiss SB2C-5 Helldiver from Bombing Squadron VB-74 crashed the barrier while landing aboard the USS *Franklin D. Roosevelt* (CVB-42, aka FDR) after a training exercise on December 12, 1945. Peacetime training could be just as tough as war and, especially around carriers, just as deadly. (USN)

Quonset's "Phil Sea" (the USS *Philippine Sea*, CV-47) returns with "duds" (three "Teebs" and three "S.B. Deucey's") after training exercises on June 14, 1946. "Duds" were aircraft too beat up by operations to fly off the carrier. Most went to A&R, although some went to Quonset's Bone Yard and the smelter. (USN)

Live firing training exercises required live targets. Quonset's Utility Squadrons, VJ-15, then "old" VU-5 followed by VJ-4/VU-4 DET, provided target tugs in the form of TBM-3J and TBM-3U "Teebs," JD-1 Douglas Invader "Jig Dogs," and, as seen here in an unusually modern blue-yellow-red scheme, Martin JM-2 Marauders. Shown here is JM-2 buno 91973 4-J-21 of VJ-4. (Bowers)

Quonset's VU-5 also provided high-speed air-launched drones as targets for ships and planes. Pictured here is a Grumman F7F-2D drone launch and control aircraft with a brace of Globe KD2G-2 drones. (USN/NA)

Quonset's World War II intensive training of Royal Navy aviators was commemorated on August 19, 1947, when Captain F.W.W. Wootten, RN, Fleet Air Arm, presented a plaque to Quonset Skipper/ComNabONE Oscar A. Weller, USN. (USN/PC)

Comfair Quonset trained more than 20 Royal Navy Squadrons and equipped them with factory-fresh top-line American built Lend-Lease aircraft, including F4F/FM Grumman/Eastern Wildcats, Curtiss SB2C Helldivers, Vought Corsairs, and, as seen here, Grumman/Eastern TBF/TBM Avengers . . . lots and lots of Avengers. (Grumman/Lovisolo)

NAS Quonset GCA saves the day for the Air Force. On October 24, 1949, a maximum effort Aerial Review was launched from Otis Air Force Base that consisted of no fewer than 36 F-84B and F-84C Republic Thunderjets of the 33rd Fighter Group to honor the dedication of the United Nations Building in New York City. The entire group became lost in fog during the return flight to Otis and, now dangerously low on fuel, the Air Force reluctantly called on Quonset radar for help. The GCA watch brought in the entire group without mishap, although several of the jets flamed-out and had to be towed from the runway! It was that close. (USAF F-84E/Curry)

Saving people's bacon was nothing new to Quonset's Ground Control Approach (GCA) Unit. Back on December 23, 1942, Quonset became the world's first GCA-equipped airfield. Only nine days later, it completed its first emergency GCA landings when a flight of PBYs was successfully "talked in" during a blinding snow storm. (USN/Quonset Scout)

Airborne radar-assisted night (N) and all-weather (AW) equipment and combat tactics development continued at Quonset after the war. Quonset's *Saipan* was assigned to Commander, Operational Development Force, Atlantic (OPDEVFORLANT, and there was no "PAC" or Pacific equivalent) and CVLG-1 during the spring of 1947. Shown here is a Quonset-developed APS-6 radar-equipped F6F-5N Hellcat of VF-1L, in *Saipan's* livery. (USN/Lawson)

The SA-317, TBM-3W AEW "Teeb" of sister squadron VA-1L, equipped with giant, Quonset-developed APS-20 radar, was also in *Saipan's* livery. On December 20, 1948, both squadrons and Light Carrier Air Group One were disestablished. Elements from these formations were merged to form "new" Development Squadron Three (VX-3) at NAS Atlantic City. VX-3 continued to operate aboard *Saipan*. (USN/Lawson)

Coast Guard SAR DET (Search and Rescue Detachment) continued to fly PBY-5As from Quonset after the war. When the bow turret was removed, radar and drop tanks were added for long-range SAR work. (USCG)

Quonset's own NATU (Naval Aircraft Torpedo Unit) was one of the Navy's first helicopter operators in 1945. When not chasing torpedoes, Sikorsky HNS-1, equipped with rescue hoist, was called on for close-in SAR. HNS-1 "40" buno 39040 was Army R-4B-SI AAF serno 43-46525. (Sikorsky)

More capable naval helicopters soon came along like this "old VX-3" Sikorsky H03S-1 XC, shown here being secured after landing upon an experimental landing platform superimposed over tried and true seaplane catapults just aft of a heavy cruiser's main battery. (Sikorsky)

The USS *Macon* (CA-132), an Oregon City-class heavy cruiser, is underway with VX-3 H03S-1 on her temporary helicopter deck. Experiments with helos aboard non-aviation ships were highly successful. Soon, cruisers and battleships lost their catapults and seaplanes. On April 1, 1948, VX-3 was split up into new Helicopter Utility Squadrons, HU-1 and HU-2 at NAS Lakehurst. (Sikorsky)

The USS *Sicily* (CVE-118) normally trained and did development work in the fixed wing ASW environment, often with Escort Carrier Group Two, which was reformed into VC-22 and later VS-22 with TBM-3S and TBM-3W Striker and Guppy teams. Here, exercises are conducted with a huge M-class airship. The Navy still considered its lighter-than-air element as a potent sub-hunter well into the 1950s. (USN/NHC)

This school of fleet-type "river boats" from New London acted as friendly enemies for Quonset aircraft during ASW exercises. An M-class ship appears at two o'clock. NAS Quonset Point's ASW mission, somewhat dormant after victory in the Battle of the Atlantic, was about to come into sharp focus. (USN)

Three

CURTAIN OF IRON OPPOSED

The first line of defense against a growing Russian submarine menace in the North Atlantic was Quonset's and ComFair Quonset's Patrol Squadrons (VPs). Pictured here is the VP-7 crew on the ramp before Seaplane Hangar Two (their home) practicing a ditching drill before an over-ocean ASW patrol. (USN/NA)

Hound Dog Seven blasts off! Patrol Squadron Eight (VP-8), a former PBM-5 Martin Mariner Medium Seaplane Squadron, VP (MS)-1, arrived at Quonset's Seaplane Side during 1948 without aircraft and was designated Medium Land Plane Patrol Squadron Eight, VP (ML)-8. Due to slow delivery of Lockheed P2V-2s, the squadron learned the land plane trade in Neptunes borrowed from sister squadron, Quonset's VP (ML)-7. Both squadrons were soon redesignated as VPs, Patrol Squadrons. Pictured here, in 1949, in one of its very own P2V-2 Neptunes, a Hound Dog crew uses JATO to launch for a training exercise in the Carib. (USN/VP-8)

Hound Dogs at sea appear in this photo along with P2V-2 Neptune aviators from Quonset's VP-8 for survival training in front of their home, Seaplane Hangar Three, after a rain squall, much to the delight of the assembled masses (squadron chiefs and sailors). VP-8 P2V-2 HD-10 bears silent witness. A known flood plain, this area is now (1998) being considered as a commercial container storage facility for the Rhode Island Port of Quonset. (USN/NA)

The potential of successful ASW got a big shot in the arm with the application of AN/APS-20 radar to both land- and carrier-based fleet aircraft. Quonset's VX-4, operating under OPDEVFORLANT, flew its nine Boeing PB-1W flying radar stations from Seaplane Hangar One. After proving its abilities in detecting friendly subs in Rhode Island waters, VX-4 mounted Operation HADDOCK, demonstrating to British Navy and RAF Coastal Command top brass the PB-1W/APS-20 radar combination's ability to detect illusive snorkel submarines in the open ocean. (USN/Schier)

VX-4's work at Quonset included AEW, airborne CIC, plus hurricane hunting, and was a direct result of World War II's Project Cadillac (see Volume I). VX-4 had buckets of experienced talent as exemplified by squadron chiefs in whites in front of PB-1W XD-40, still sporting its World War II chin turret sans .50 caliber guns. (USN/Boober)

31

All manner of radar development continued at Quonset commands under the Iron Curtain threat. Project MICKEY and NAVY WHITE began at Beavertail Point, shown here, and continued into the late 1950s. (MIT Museum)

MICKEY and Quonset's Project AFIRM, later redesignated as NACTULANT, then VC(N)-2), helped develop equipment for all of the Navy's night and early all-weather fighters. The radar operator's post in Grumman F7F-2N night fighters was used by Marines. (Grumman/Lovisolo)

Quonset's NATU, homeported in Seaplane Hangar One, developed torpedo gear for the Grumman F7F-2N night fighter. (Grumman/Lovisolo)

Good drop! NATU aircraft frequented the Newport Torpedo Station's East Passage firing ranges on an almost daily basis, developing both anti-surface and anti-submarine weapons. Here, 4-NATU, AD-2 Douglas Skyraider buno 122355 is out earning its pay. On May 1, 1951, eight Navy ADs from the USS *Princeton* (CV-37), with great precision and determination, successfully used anti-ship torpedoes against the Hwachon hydroelectric dam in Korea. (USN/Barthelmes)

NAS Quonset Point and Comfair Quonset continued to equip and train Carrier Air Groups in the old CVBG-75 F4U-4 Corsairs aboard the *FDR* (USN) . . .

. . . and the new ECM AD-2Q Skyraiders from VC-33 (NA-12 in foreground), HU-2 H03S-1 plane guard Fleet Angel turned up aft aboard the *FDR*. (USN/Lawson)

34

ADs at angels ten from CVBG-3 over the USS *Midway* (CVB-41). (USN)

VC-4 AD-1Q NA-7 goes into the barrier and noses up. Sudden engine stoppage like this created great stresses in the airframe and usually meant an overhaul at Quonset's A&R (redesignated O&R, Overhaul and Repair Department) before a Skyraider could once again embrace the sky. (USNI/Lawson)

Disaster! An explosion and resulting $5 million fire enveloped O&R's Engine Shop shortly after 3 p.m. on October 15, 1948. All hands, Navy and civilian, instantly turned to rescuing trapped, injured, helpless personnel. (USN)

Within a year, all would be well as the Navy erected a brand new Engine Shop that could build both piston and jet power plants, the first of its kind in the service. This gang, pictured in Fuselage Shop, is all smiles, proud of their work, as they pose in front of a stripped-out JRF-5 Grumman Goose amphibian tucked into the AD line. (USN/Blouin)

On New Year's Eve 1949, a big Nor'easter blew in, causing damage to the naval air station, especially at the Carrier Pier. Diving Tender YDT-2 was sunk at her berth after being crushed by a runaway civilian barge. YDT-2 was used in company with Seaplane Wrecking Derricks (YSDS, seen aft) to recover remains of crashed Quonset aircraft. (USN/NA)

This peacetime view was taken from Quonset Tower on October 19, 1949. The object to the right of the tower is a new height-finding radar. The speck on the water near the Crash Boat House is PBM-5 landing on the Seadrome. Lines of AD's, Corsairs, and a few TBMs on the Paint Shop Ramp await induction into the O&R Plant. The Paint Shop Hangar is now the location of the Quonset Air Museum. The Paint Shop Ramp now displays more than 27 of the museum's historic aircraft, including several that actually served at Quonset. Go visit! (USN/NA)

37

During the 1949 "Admirals' Revolt," Quonset almost got the chop from the newly formed Defense Department, which favored very large "strategic bombers" over the proven aircraft carriers. The ten-engined Convair B-36 fully embodied this faulty doctrine. Here, Convair GRB-36F-CF Project TOM TOM with a RF-84F Thunderflash recon jet is playing the part of parasite escort fighter that was to hook on to the wing tip of *Mother Peacemaker* for the long trip to Moscow. Sure. (Convair)

Meanwhile, worthwhile proven concepts and projects within the Naval Aviation family languished and died. One of these was America's first super carrier, the USS *United States* (CVA-58). Well along to launching, she was killed by the Truman administration, stillborne, right in her graving dock. Note nuclear capable P2C-3C Neptunes and FH-1 jet fighters on the flight deck of this artist's concept of CVA-58. (USN/Rausa)

As the nation optimistically approached the decade of the 1950s, Quonset's aviation assets helped with the evaluation of captured ships, such as this advanced TYPE XXI Nazi EX-U3008 streamlined snorkler. The USSR also carefully studied their hi-tech German spoils-of-war and quickly developed an undersea threat to the world's democracies that Quonset would defend against for the rest of her operational life as a naval air station. (NA/NHC)

Against this threat, the Navy's carriers could field only World War II relics like this TBM-3E with older, short-range, APS-6 radar. TBM-3W2 Guppies with long-range, accurate APS-20 radar were entering the fleet but in small numbers and mostly going to Attack Carriers, as few were spared for deployment aboard ASW-dedicated CVE Escort Carriers. (Grumman/Lovisolo)

Ashore, the Navy did have the highly capable and powerful P2V series, but most lacked the crucial APS-20 radar with which to hunt snorkel boats. A few P2V-3Ws had this gear, but it was not until the P4V-4 series that the APS-20 became standard equipment. Here, the Fairwing Three P2V-2 crew pays the ultimate price for maintaining their nation's "peacetime" freedom. (USN/NA)

Neptune buno 122454 burned to the ground. Heroic but failed efforts of Quonset sailors to save the aft crew resulted in severe burns, and, later, the Navy and Marine Corps Medal. The date of this crash was June 1, 1950. Within less than four weeks, things would begin to really heat up for many more Quonset flying sailors. (USN/NA)

Four

KOREA

"I will go to Korea," said Republican Presidential candidate Dwight David Eisenhower, retired General of the Army. Bound for Korea, a F4U-5N Corsair night fighter of VC-4 buno 124478 is loaded aboard the USS *Lake Champlain* (CV-39) at the Quonset Carrier Pier (USN/NA)

Quonset's CAG-3 was one of the first to join in the battle when the Korean War broke out on June 25, 1950. Aboard the *Leyte*, CAG-3 in chopped Korea on October 9, 1950. Often in terrible winter weather, CAG-3 flew strikes in support of the Pusan Perimeter, the Invasion of Wonson, the Hungnam Salient, and strikes on the Yalu River Bridges (the real "Bridges at Toko Ri"). The driver of VA-35 AD-3 K-505 made it. Just! (USN/NA)

Carrier Air Group Three's War Cruise to Korea generated many true heroes. VF-32 Corsair pilot LTJG Thomas Jerome Hudner Jr. received the Congressional Medal Honor for intentionally crash landing his F4U in an attempt to save his squadron mate, ENS Jesse Brown, America's first black Naval Aviator, who was trapped in his Corsair's cockpit after being shot down on December 14, 1950. Despite heroic efforts by Hudner and Marine helicopter pilot Charley Ward (VMO-6), Jesse didn't make it. (USN/NAVNews)

Composite Squadrons VC-4 and VC-33 were both attached to CAG-3 and the *Leyte* during the War Cruise. Often working together, they delivered powerful strikes against the enemy day *and night*. The AD-2Qs (SS) and F4U-5Ns (NA) pictured here returned to the *Leading Lady* after interdiction mission against reinforcements flowing in from Manchuria, on November 7, 1950. (USN/NA)

A night fighting VC-4 F4U-5N NA-38 joins stack forward after a successful mission and trap. Quonset's Composite Squadron Twelve (VC-12) DET was also with CAG-3 in their AEW AD-W Guppies. This photo was taken November 7, 1950. (USN/NA)

Quonset s CAG-7 in chopped Korea aboard the USS *Bon Homme Richard* (CVA-31) on June 21, 1952, and immediately took on North Korean and Chinese Communist forces. During a grueling six-month War Cruise, CAG-7 killed 4,086 enemy troops and destroyed 1,123 vehicles, 828 railway cars, 20 locomotives, 24 tanks, 131 gun emplacements, and 68 bridges. The CAG-7 seen here was on a NATO training exercise aboard the *Midway* in the Med with VR-22 TBM-3R CODs launching aft, November 1, 1951. (USN/NA)

CAG-7 was made up of VF-71 and VF-72 in F9F Panther jets, VF-74 in Corsairs, and VA-75 in AD-4s. Attached to CAG-7 were Composite Squadrons VC-4, VC-12, VC-33, and VC-61 (photo) from NAS Mirimar. CAG-7's first Korean War combat actions were against hydroelectric complexes and Pyongyang in North Korea. Pictured here is VC-4 with rare F2H-2N (NA-95) buno 123307 and trusty F4U-5N (NA-58). (USN/Lawson)

VC-4 DET in chopped Korea aboard the USS *Lake Champlain* (CVA-39) with CAG-4 on June 10, 1953. They carqualed in their F3D-2 "Skynights" while underway to the combat area—quite an achievement. In this photo, NA-71 comes aboard. (USN/Lawson)

Pictured here are pilots of a VC-4 DET in front of F3D-2 NA-74. Korean War work included night and bad weather escort of USAF B-29 bomber formations (the Air Force needed lots of help in this area) and night interdiction while based ashore in Korea, right in the combat zone. (USN/Geary)

Supporting these war operations back at Quonset was Fasron Two installing radar equipment, IFF, armor plate . . . you name it, to help prepare all squadrons for combat. Extensive combat training was provided by Quonset's new utility squadron, VU-2, which provided fast tow targets as well as "friendly enemy" fighter aircraft. The VU-2 "Jig Dog" UJ-5 here is ready to start engines. TBM-3U UJ-38 is in the background. (VU-2/Brooks)

Comfair's Fleet Angels also went to Korea and rescued many aircrews right in hostile territory. HU-2 also performed other tasks in addition to combat rescue. This HU-2 H03S-1 UR-41 from the light cruiser USS *Worchester* (CA-144) arrived on the British carrier HMS *Theseus* for mine-spotting duty. (Royal Navy)

HU-2 H03S-1 UR-42 delivers guard mail to a U.S. Navy cruiser underway. (Sikorsky)

This was the insignia of HU-2 Fleet Angels during the time of the Korean War. (HU-2)

Back in Rhode Island, Quonset's Fairwing Three provided heavy, long-range patrol planes for the Second Fleet (Atlantic Ocean), the Sixth Fleet (the Med), and ComFair Quonset. Composed of six Patrol Squadrons and several Fasrons, Wing home ports included Quonset, VP-7, VP-8, VP-11, Fasron-101, Pax River VP-21, VP-24, Fasron-103, Argentia, Newfoundland VP-3, and Fasron-106. Pictured here is the P4M-1 Mercator HC-7 of VP-21. (Williams)

VP-11 P4Y-2 HB Privateer with VP-21 "How Charming SEVEN" alongside at Pax. VP-11 did long-range patrols and some ASW. VP-21 in the unique P4M-1s had a special night, fast, low-level, heavy-mining mission in the Med to bottle up the Russian Black Sea Fleet. The P4M had two jets, as well as two prop engines, and was the *best* VP type aircraft of the period. (Dickey/Lawson)

48

This is the VP-24 P4Y-2B HA-9 Bat Missile-capable Privateer. This squadron had a special anti-ship mission. (USN/USNI)

Pictured here is the VP-21 HC-2 P4M-1 buno 124363. The Navy, especially VP-21, was very pleased with the big Martins, but limited production kept the cost of the Mercator high at $1.8 million. For that, the Navy could and did buy two-and-a-half P2V Neptunes! It is a beautiful ship, though. (USN/Curry)

After Korean combat, CAG-3 and the *Leyte* returned to Quonset but soon shoved off for a refreshing Med cruise. (USN/CVA-32)

Korean War Composite Squadron brothers were back aboard the *Leading Lady* too. Here, joyful airdales of VC-33 pull an engine check on AD-4N SS-801. (USN/CVA-32)

Back at Quonset, Carrier Air Anti-Submarine warfare ground on day and night. It was tough, dangerous, and usually thankless *work*. The USS *Salerno Bay* loaded up a VS-32 TBM-3S Stricker on November 2, 1951. Ship and squadron later participated in ASW Exercise CONVEX III in the Caribbean operating area. (USN)

HU-2's first HUP-1, UR-50, deployed with Quonset's VS-31 aboard the USS *Siboney* CVE-112. Both squadrons were in the Navy's latest equipment. VS-31 was the first with AF-2S and AF-2W Guardians, and HU-2 was the first in the fleet with the Piasecki Hups. HU-2 got the better deal. (USN/HU-2)

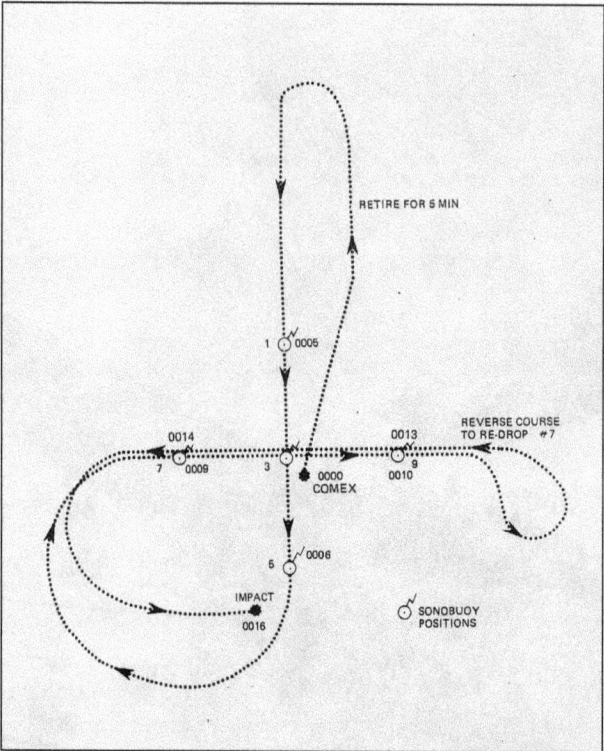

This was a typical sonobouy drop pattern flown by Quonset's ASW VS squadrons during the 1950s and 1960s. Flying low and slow, 150 feet at 130 knots, day and night over the dark and stormy North Atlantic while trying to achieve a tight pattern was tedious, demanding, dangerous labor. More than one Quonset crew flew right into the water while concentrating on hunting the elusive and stealthy Russian subs. (USN/TG BRAVO)

The VS-913 AF-2S Guardian SN-4 buno 126784 returned to Quonset Carrier Pier. Due to a failed GCA, it flew into water .75 miles from the naval air station. There were no survivors from this accident on November 10, 1952. (USN/NA/Webster)

This VS-39 AF-2W Guardian crashed at night December 20, 1954. There were no survivors. (USN/NA)

Pictured here is an AF-2W Guardian. Landing the Navy's widest carrier plane (almost 61 foot wing span) on its narrowest flight decks (the CVE "jeep" carriers, which were 80 feet wide) could be rugged. A very hard landing caused the engine to break off, but the crew survived. (USN/Chinfo)

All is well with the VS-31 Hunter Killer (HUK) Team. Shown here is the AF-2W SP-11 Guppy with the SP-2 AF-2S Stricker over a New London Fleet-type "River Boat." (USN/Lawson)

The AF-2W SL-18 from VS-22 got a good cat shot from Rhode Island namesake USS *Block Island* (CVE-106). (USN/NA)

Shown here is "the Block" underway with AF-2W and AF-2S Guardians from VS-24. (USN/USNI)

The small size of an ASW "jeep" carrier is evident here as the USS *Salerno Bay* (CVE-110) lines up with Fleet Oiler USS *Allogash* (AO-97) for underway replenishment. On the flight deck are three F4U-5Ns from VC-4 and seven TBM-3S Strikers plus five TBM-3W Guppies. Fleet oilers and other replenishment ships are, and always have been, <u>indispensable</u> for our carrier Navy. (USN)

Quonset's axle deck "Miss T" (USS *Tarawa* CVS-40) was straight as a razor. "Building 40s" V-1 Division carefully inspects cross deck pendants before the next recovery. Missing the wires and the barrier would send one straight into the stack forward. Things were about to change. (USN)

America's first angled deck carrier, the USS *Antietam* (CVS-36), had Quonset as her first home port after her epoch metamorphosis. She is shown here on January 14, 1953. (USN)

Five

THE COLD WAR AND THE NEW NAVY

The new Navy! Pictured here are Hoot Owls of Quonset's top notch ASW squadron. VS-39 shows how its done over Narragansett Bay in 1958. Tight formation flying in the very close coupled Stoof S2Fs was rare, difficult, and a bit dangerous if anyone suddenly lost an engine. No matter, the former Reserve Squadron from Squantum (VS-913) could do anything! (USN/VS-32/Snow)

Quonset's VP-8 Hound Dogs show formation flying skills in their shiny new, three-gun turreted, P2V-5 Neptunes, c. 1953. VP-8, and sister squadron VP-7, deployed all over the North Atlantic Ocean as well as the Caribbean and Mediterranean operating areas that included Roosevelt Roads, Guantanimo, Argentina, Goose Bay, Thule, Kelavik, Rota, Port Lyautey, Malta, and Crete. VP-7 went to Korea, just before the cease fire. (USN/VP-8)

By July 31, 1955, VP-8 had traded in its last two heavily armed "straight" P2V-5s for the new, jet engine-augmented P2V-5F (note Westinghouse J-34 pods under wings). The new tail code "LC" came along between July 24, 1956, and June 1, 1957 per OPNAVINST. (USN/Webster)

VP-21 also received new aircraft as they turned over their unique P4M-1 Mercators for Lockheed P2V-6 Neptunes. The six version had a longer bomb bay for mining, which was the squadron's main business. The P2V-6 also had large 420-gallon tip tanks of the P2V-5 and full gun turret installations. VP-21 aircrews were disappointed with this Neptune due to cramped crew stations and lack of auxiliary jets. In this photo, the P2V-6 AIRMAIL-4 plane captain is ready to go. (VP-21/Williams)

Comfair's "Fleet Angels" also received a new helo in the form of the ultimate "egg beater," the Kaman HUK-1. Built in small numbers in nearby Moosup, Connecticut, the side-by-side, intermeshing, counter-rotating system worked well, although it was difficult to keep the wooden rotors dry as they soaked up moisture like a sponge, causing the blades to go out of balance. HUK-1s, like the one shown here, HUK-1 HU-71 buno 145312, finished their days ashore. (USN/HU-2)

This Jules Verne-looking apparition, A2D-1 Buno 125481, is the fantastic Douglas Skyshark. Had they gone into production, Quonset was to be the Overhaul Head for this 5,000-horsepower brute. Only eight were built, with two production versions (bunos 125482 and 125484) ending up at Quonset O&R for unknown reasons (other than perhaps as pilot aircraft to start an A2D-1 production line) during the fall of 1956. (Douglas/Gann)

Quonset's O&R personnel had little to worry about as the Douglas Skyhawk—the inspired work of Mr. Attack Aviation himself, Ed Heinemann—had just come aboard. Quonset was designated as the Overhaul Head for this magnificent bantam. Quonset's VA-72 was the first squadron in the Navy to receive the A4D-1 "Scooter" on September 27, 1956. VA-72 L-210 buno 139944 is shown here. (Douglas/Gann)

This pilot of Quonset's Fighting Squadron Seventy-Three is on top of the world in October 1956 as he stands by to mount his beautifully tricked out FJ-3 Fury jet. On the bottom of the world, old prop JigDog ex-Army light bombers of Quonset's Utility Squadron Two (VU-2) in the background towed targets for the fighter jocks and tin can sailors. (USN/VU-2/Brooks)

One of the Navy's last FJ-3M Fury fighters, buno 141435 L-313 from Quonset's CAG Seven VF-73, taxis forward after a good trap. After FJs disappeared from carriers, J-65 production at Quonset's Engine Shop continued without missing a beat as A4Ds used the same basic power plant as did USAF B-57 light bombers, for which Quonset also supplied engines. (USN/Lawson)

An AD-4NA (P)S-502 believed to be from VA-55 appears in this photo, burning after landing on the flight deck of the USS *Essex* (CVA-9). The *Essex* was cruising off the coast of Vietnam during the Viet Minh's final attacks against French Legionnaires making a last ditch defense of Dien Bien Phu. If Ike had decided to come to the aid of the French Colonialists, the *Essex* would have been ordered to go in. After Project 125 conversion to angle deck, the *Essex* came to Quonset as-CVS-9. (USN)

Former Reserve AD-4NL 7Y-164 from NART Grosse Ile awaits its fate at the Navy Bone Yard, NAF Litchfield Park. During late 1959, the Navy began pulling some older ADs out of mothballs for various projects, including checking out pilots of the Republic of Vietnam Air Force (RVNAF) and supplying them with revived Skyraiders. Instructors from the Navy's AD Advanced Training Unit (ATU-301) showed them how to do so. Skyraiders resurrected at Quonset gave them something to fly. Stripped of all night and cold weather gear, AD-4NLs became AD-4NAs (A-1Ds), the first ADs to fight in Vietnam. (USN)

Quonset's FASRON-2 helped Fleet Squadrons with the maintenance and modification of many types of aircraft. Gleaming, bare metal, a Vought F7U-3 Cutlass XC-01 up from new VX-3 was a rarity. Commander Art Tarabusi, USNR, designer of the Lincoln sedan, flew the Cutlass in. Quonset was scheduled to be the Overhaul Head for F7Us. (Tarabusi)

FASRON-2 also helped the Royal Canadian Navy (RCN) with their "new" F2H-3 Banshees. Starting on November 25, 1955, the RCN's VX-10 (Experimental Squadron Ten) began taking delivery on several dozen F2H-3 "Big Banjos," which America was transferring to its northern ally. Most came directly from deployments and other fleet duty, and were in tough shape. Fasron and O&R got the Canadians safely on their way. B/N 126414 is shown here. (RCN)

Mishaps right on board the naval air station provided plenty of bent aluminum for Overhaul to care for. VP-8 P2V-5F buno 127738 came to blows with VS-39 S2F-1 buno 133044 on May 29, 1956. (USN/Chinfo)

VA(AW)-33 Nighthawks' AD-5W Guppy came to grief when it hit emergency arresting gear rigged on the wrong end of the runway. A lesser plane than the ole' AD would have folded up. (Author)

By day . . . this was the VC-4 AD-4Q NA-632 buno 124044. (USN/Lawson)

. . . and by night, VF(AW)-4 AD-5 NA-608 buno 132452. (USN/ Lawson)

This VC-4 personnel inspection took place at NAS Atlantic City. When NBB closed in 1958, this squadron, redesignated as VF(AW)-4, moved to its new home port—Quonset Point. (USN/VF(AW)-4)

Pictured here is the VF(AW)-4 AD-5 GC-36 (not a Nan) with AN/APS-19 radar on port wing rolling for deck launch. During the late 1950s, VF(AW)-4 deployed DETS of AD-5s like this in the fighter role aboard all of Lant and Sixth Fleet CVS ASW Support Carriers. (USN/Lawson)

Fill 'er up. A VC-4 F2H-4 E-602 plugs the basket and receives fuel from an AJ-1 Savage tanker, NB-8 of VAH-5. The AJ was the original Navy carrier-based horizontal nuclear bomber. The Banshee, starting with VC-4's F2H-2Bs, was the first nuclear-capable tactical aircraft deployed on an aircraft carrier. (USN/VF(AW)-4)

Earthquake Two Three F2H-4 GC-23 buno 127588, shown here visiting MCAS El Toro, was one of the last Fleet Banjos. (Douglas/Gann)

The Great Hurricane of 1954 was not as bad as '38, but was still bad enough. Carol did a job on the air station. Although the Air Station Hurricane Bill was properly executed and all serviceable aircraft were flown inland, many top line aircraft awaiting work at O&R and the Aircraft Modification Unit (AMU) in Seaplane Hangar One were swamped and wrecked by the storm surge. The crash boat got loose and headed for Main Gate. (QS)

The Rhode Island Blizzard of '56 shut down the great naval air station for more than 12 hours. Normal industrial operations took several days to restore as the civilian work force struggled to get to work. Quonset's sailors and Marines manned hundreds of scoops, shovels, and brooms. The partially dug out Station Jay Bird (SNJ-5) Number 593 appears in this photo. (USN/Comfair)

A rare, nuclear-capable, S2F-2 Grumman Tracker flies wing on the much more proliferate brother S2F-1 from VS-32. The Quonset-based ASW squadron helped the Coast Guard with the International Ice Patrol in North Atlantic shipping lanes during the late 1950s. The sub hunters were perfect for detecting, measuring, and tracking icebergs. The Cold War need to keep track of Russian nuclear submarine menace, especially after the Cuban Missile Crisis, put an end to this most beneficial "peacetime" work. (USN/VS-32/Snow)

This photo shows a slide in the snow. A Task Group BRAVO S2F-1 managed to crash land on air station property after a mid-air collision with another Stoof attempting to land on same runway. A prop blade from other Stoof sliced into the port engine cowl. The crew of 40 survived. (USN)

Quonset's two Attack Carrier Air Groups, Korean War veterans CAG-3 and CAG-7, departed Quonset for the last time during the mid- to late 1950s as did most of Fairwing Three's elements except for VP-8 Hound Dogs. Quonset's focus now, with few exceptions, was Carrier Based Antisubmarine Warfare in the real world of the Cold War. Aboard the *Tarawa*, VS-31 S2F-1 SP-6 tensions up on port cat. (USN)

This VS-39 S2F-1 SN-6 is almost ready to go. (USN)

This VS-31 Stoof
returning from
mission taxies forward
while folding wings
to start forming the
stack. (USN)

VS-31 Top Cat and VS-39 Hoot Owl Stoofs wait to be stuck below for upkeep.

Quonset's ASW flat tops almost always brought along several Composite Squadron DETS equipped with AD Guppies for AEW, Control, and Bellhop radio relay work (VC/VAW-12), plus AD-5s or F2H-4 Banshees from VC/VF(AW)-4 for CVS Defense (to defend the carrier from air or surface attack). Sometimes an Attack Squadron DET would fulfill the latter duty. Pictured here is *Miss T* with F2H-2B DET from CAG-17's VA-172 in the Med for special operations in September/October 1957. The F2H-2B was the Navy's first nuclear-capable tactical aircraft. (USN/CVS-40)

Similar work was in store for VA-44 DET aboard the *Wasp* (CVS-18) as their F9F-8 Grumman Cougars shared the forward flight deck with a HU-2 "Fleet Angel" HUP helo from August 30 to October 22, 1957. (USN)

VC-33 deployed on all of the Navy's Atlantic Fleet and Sixth Fleet carriers, CVAs and CVSs. In this photo, an AD-4N SS-28 carquals on new angled deck of CVS-36, the USS *Antietam*, on January 14, 1953. During 1953, VC-33 had on strength eight F3D-2 jet night fighters, eleven AD-4Bs, seven AD-4NLs, twenty-one AD-4Ns, one AD-3N, one AD-4Q, one AD-3Q, and two SNB-5s. (USN)

Within a year, VC-33 had taken delivery of the much improved, four-crew AD-5N. As the squadron's mission began to encompass more and more ECM (electronic counter measures), many of these Nans were converted to electronic warfare Queens (AD-5Q). Quonset NAMU and O&R made most of the changes during major overhaul periods. Pictured here is the AD-5N SS-4 buno 132493. (Barthelmes)

Rotor heads arrived. Navy interest in helicopters as ASW platforms using dipping sonar goes back to World War II, but it was not until the mid-1950s that choppers had developed enough, in both performance and endurance, to become a viable ASW asset. The Navy had some success with the H04S-3 and the HUP-2S, but the first true ASW helo was the HSS-1. Quonset's first ASW helo Squadron HS-9 formed at the air station in 1956. (USN)

HS-9 was soon joined by HS-5. HS-9's first year included a lot of work for COMOPDEVFORLANT on the HUL-DL Project which led to the DASH drone anti-submarine helicopter plus ASW operations from the *Leyte* including NATO Exercises SEAWATCH and FEND-OFF. (USN)

Seabat's one mission: "To Detect and Destroy Enemy Submarines." The most effective use of HSS-1 dipping sonar was in the Inner Zone, working closely with destroyers. Pictured here is the newer HSS-1N with auto-pilot and better all-weather capabilities, which made the work a bit easier, although the job was still stressful and dangerous, especially at night over water. (USN/HS-5)

All Fleet Hiss One and Hiss One NAN ASW helos were rigged with a rescue hoist. Many were saved. (USN/HS-5)

"Fire in Hangar Bay ONE!" While operating with Task Group BRAVO, the USS *Wasp* suffered a serious fire after a helo engine exploded in the forward hangar deck. (USN/CVS-18)

This red-hot engine was manhandled to the side to be jettisoned. Many were burned and injured, and two men were killed. Training and true raw courage saved the day for the *Wasp*. (USN/CVS-18)

Back to hunting subs. In this photo, Quonset's Task Group BRAVO VS-31 Topcat S2F-1 MC-21 buno 136583 gets dragged to a re-spot on a slush-and-ice-covered flight deck during a winter storm in the late 1950s. Enlisted plane handlers, usually youngsters barely eighteen years old, grew up quick on days like this. (USN/VS-31)

Then home. (USN/NA)

Quonset's prime Cold War mission was support of the entire Anti-Submarine Task Group. (USN)

Six

SPACE, BUTTER, AND VIETNAM

Pictured here in September 1962, is the arrival of the presidential yacht HONEYFITZ (the USS *Sequoia*, AG-23) as the USS *Lake Champlain* (CVS-39) and her Air Group, CVSG-54, man the rail. Jack and Jackie were frequent visitors to the great naval air station on the way to her parents' abode, the Summer White House, in Newport. (USN/PC)

JFK, Jackie, and President Khan of Pakistan are greeted by ComFair Quonset, the air station Commanding officer and the president of the Naval War College, as Marine One HSS-2Z stands by. The first Presidential Lift by HMX-1's Marine One (an HUS-1Z) took place five years before at Quonset when Ike was commander in chief. (USN/PC)

Rhode Island Senior Senator John O. Pastore is greeted by NAS Quonset's Commanding officer, Captain Hardaker, and ComFair Quonset's Chief of Staff, Captain David C. Rains. Senatore Pastore always had a great interest in the naval air station and fought hard for its survival. (USN/PC)

Pictured here are the "Missiles of October." As President Kennedy imposed the quarantine of Cuba, Quonset's ASW Carrier Air Groups, Squadrons, and the USS *Essex* (CVS-9) were on station, patrolling for Russian ships loaded with the IRBM nuclear missiles and IL-28 tactical nuclear bombers that the USSR had supplied to Cuba. (USN)

HSS-1 ASW helo from CVSG over a Russian sub off Cuba. (USN)

Run-ins with the Russians and Quonset's flying sailors continued during the early 1960s Cold War, as Russian Badger bombers shadowed and sometimes over flew our carriers in international waters. This was one reason that VF-type aircraft were sometimes deployed aboard Quonset's ASW Carriers. (USN)

Quonset's USS *Essex* made a port call while on MIDLINK SIX Med cruise with CVSG-60 aboard: VS-39, VS-34, HS-9, and Marine Corps H&MS-32 Sub Unit One with four A4D-2 (A-4B) Skyhawk jet attack aircraft. The sole function of this detachment, the first ever from a Marine Headquarters Squadron, was CVS *Defense*. Equipped with 20-mm loads and AIM-9 Sidewinder heat seeking missiles, the Marines kept the bad guys away from the *Essex*. (USN)

On the way home from the Med, during a horrific North Atlantic winter storm, the *Essex's* 20-ton mast snapped and came crashing down on the Marine Scooters December 21, 1963. (USN/Chinfo)

This view from Vultures Row shows Fly One all smashed up. No one was killed. The ship may have rolled over if the mast didn't snap. One of the A4Ds was a Strike. This was the first Marine jet ever shot down by a maneuvering Navy mast. The *Essex* limped home under partial power and made the Carrier Pier on the day before Christmas Eve. All hands had much to be thankful for. The next day, the old war horse actually sank alongside the Carrier Pier. (USN/Chinfo)

On a better day, the *Essex* steamed as ASW Task Group Flagship. The smart-looking CVL light carrier is the HMCS *Bonaventure*. Destroyers included the *Decatur* (DD-936) and the *Sullivans* (DD-537), both out of Newport. The small SSK Guppy-type sub is the USS *Argonaut* (SS-475). She was later turned over to the Canadians as the HMCS *Rainbow* (SS 75). (USN/CVSG-60)

Royal Canadian Navy ships and air squadrons frequently operated with NAS Quonset's forces and occasionally made port calls at the air station. Under Comfair, Joint ASW Exercises included air work with Naval Reserve formations as Canadian CS2F-1 DeHaviland-built Grumman Tracker 567 joined up on NAS South Weymouth S2F-1 7Z-171 buno 136537. (USN)

It seems that Quonset's old straight deck *Champ* was busy as heck and could do just about anything in the 1960s. During the summer of 1962, she operated a 15-plane squadron of massive Marine heavy lift helos, Sikorsky HR2S-1s from HMH-461, MCAS New River. As shown in this photo, Squadron Deuce, CJ-6 buno 140324, is landing aboard the USS *Valley Forge* (CVS-45). The *Happy Valley* became LPH-8, an Amphibious Assault Carrier, in 1961. (USN/HMH-461)

This Deuce, a big bullfrog-looking eyesore, is one of the two Sikorsky HR2S-1W airborne early warning (AEW) test helicopters based on the Marine's HR 2S-1 Mojave heavy lifter, equipped with the huge, Quonset-proven, APS-20E radar. The aircraft flew okay despite its outrageous radar dome, but the big twin piston-engined Deuce, a known rattler, was too tough an environment for all those vacuum tubes. With more durable equipment two decades later, the Royal Navy adopted AEW helicopters after hard lessons learned in the Falklands War. If they had gone into production, Quonset was to have been the HR2S-1W Overhaul Head. (buno 141646/Sikorsky)

NAS Quonset Point remained fully operational as a Seadrome through the mid-1960s. The last seaplane ops were in the early 1960s with P5M-2 Martin Marlin giant flying boats during ASW Exercises. The only thing left at Quonset with a boat hull that could fly was Quonset Fleet Air Detachment UF-2G amphibian Albatross with Navy and Coast Guard crew. Thus closed the seaplane tradition that began at the air station on December 20, 1940. (USN/Curry)

Quonset's last land-based Patrol Squadron also departed. This VP-8 P3V-1 gets a freshwater bath at NAS Brunswick. Still a component of ComFair Quonset, VP-8 was the first squadron in the Navy to receive the highly advanced turboprop P3V-1 Lockheed Orion. (USN)

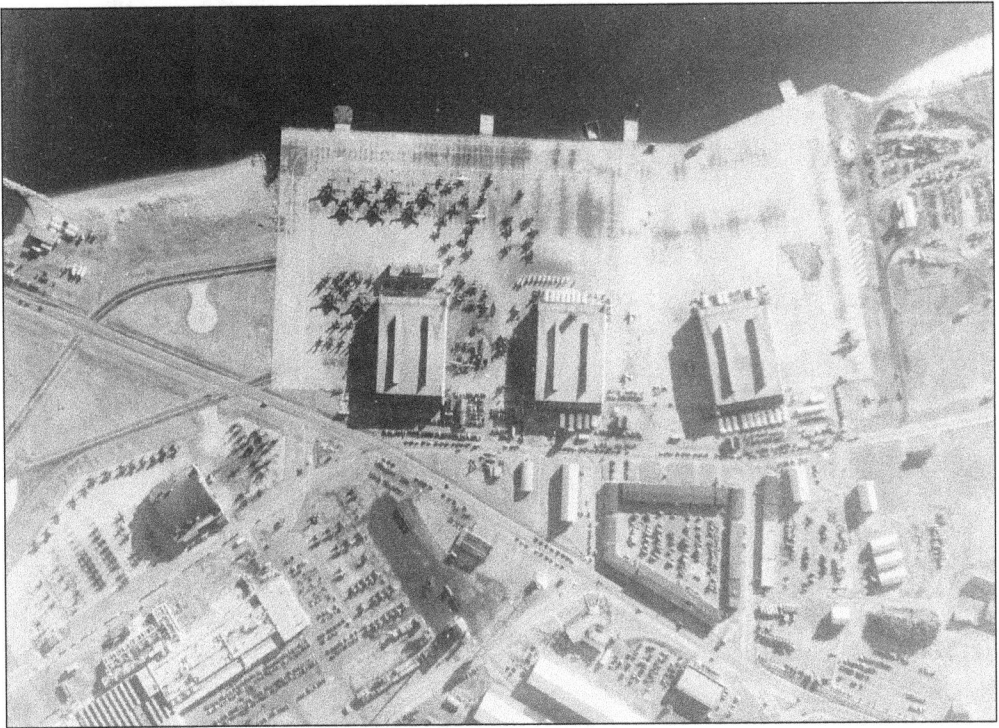

VP-8's departure provided more space on the usually cramped Seaplane Side. (USN)

Operating from Seaplane Hangar One (SPH-1) along with NAMU, NATU got temporary relief. This was especially appreciated by crews laboring on NATU's largest asset, P2V-5F 2-NATU, buno 127780. (USN/NATU)

This NATU inspection took place on one of those cold, gray, misty Quonset mornings. Note the torpedo rack outboard port jet. (USN/NATU)

Torpedo Unit's sharp, polished bare metal, A4D-1 and 1-NATU, S2F-1, was ready to join for formation flight. (USN/NATU)

This 4-NATU HSS-LN buno 143895 lifted from SPH-1 ramp crowded with NAMU ADs. (USN/NATU/Golder)

Pictured here is a 1-NATU S2F-1 buno 133219 with Torp Unit insignia on the nose and weapons bay open. (Author)

Seaplane Side crowding resumed when the first HS-9, and then HS-5, received the new, Greyhound Bus-sized Sikorsky HSS-2 Sea King. HS-9 HSS-2s followed by HS-5 HSS-1s was ready to turn up in front of SPH-3. (USN/Curry)

The HS-9 HSS-2 AW-63 is pictured here with its rotors turning. (USN/Curry)

This is the HS-9 HS-9 AW-52 buno 149004, rolling. (USN/HS-9)

Since its establishment at Quonset in 1948, VAW-12 had always called the air station its home port. Its AD Guppies were a fixture around the Seaplane Side and, in terms of shear numbers of aircraft assigned, VAW-12 was often cited as the largest squadron in the Navy. AD-5W GE-734 is shown here. (USN/VAW-12)

Then, in 1962, VAW-12 began to transition into the new, big, twin-engine WF-2 Grumman Tracer. (USN)

Since space was at a premium, VAW-12 packed up and took its WF-2 "Fudds" to NAS Norfolk. (USN)

VAW-33 remained on the Seaplane Side and inherited all of VAW-12 AD-5W Guppies and their missions. Thirty-Three was now responsible for all prop ECM DETs on the Navy's East Coast attack carriers and all of the control and communications relay work on the ASW support carriers. (USN/Barthelmes)

When it was found that operating the WF-2s from the CVSs was pushing the envelope too much on hangar deck spaces and flight deck spots, VAW-33 was also tasked with supplying DETs to all Atlantic and Sixth Fleet Support Carriers. The beautiful AD-5 with plush interior was the squadron's own COD (Carrier Onboard Delivery) and flew everywhere delivering squadron personnel and vital spare parts to the DETS at sea. (Author)

The Navy's Antarctic Development Squadron, VX-6, was home-ported at Quonset for more than 15 years and flew a wonderful variety of aircraft. This is the DeHaviland UC-1 otter buno 144672 JD-14 on the ramp in front of its off-ice home, Land Plane Hangar Four (LPH-4) in May 1961. (Author)

Over the ice, VX-6 UC-1 JD-15 flew helicopter support, logistics, and parachute drop missions.

This photo was taken at Quonset in May 1961, and shows a ski-equipped P2V-7LP JD-1. The object on the jet pod is a kangaroo. When on the ice, the patrol bomber photo mapped the entire Antarctic Continent and flew logistics missions. Note the larger 420-gallon tip tank, sans searchlight, of P2V-5. The size of the old Man of the Sea can be gauged by the squadron's half ton Ford. (Author)

On the ice, salamanders keep R5D-3 JD-5 engines warm. (USN/VX-6)

This is an R4D-5L JD-8 buno 17239. Squadron R4D-5L *Que Sera Sera* made the first landing at the South Pole. It now resides at the National Museum of Naval Aviation in Pensacola. (USN/VX-6)

This photo shows an R4D-8L JD-10 with engine covers. (USN/VX-6)

An R4D-8L JD-9 buno 17219 off-loads cargo onto a motorized sledge. (USN/VX-6)

This is the ultimate Antarctic explorer, the VX-6 Lockheed Hercules C-130BL JD-21. In 1999, VXE-6 will hand over its ski-equipped "Herks" to the USAF and civilian operators as the Navy retires its "Puckered Penguins." (USN/ VX-6)

Helping Hand. Cdr. Alan B. Shepard, Jr., USN, the first American astronaut to go into space, is the recipient on completing his 116-mile-high, 302-mile-long flight in the Project Mercury "Free-dom 7" capsule, 5 May 1961. In a classic example of team effort, the recovery was made by Marine Corps Helicopter Squadron HMR(L)-262, operating from the USS *Lake Champlain* (CVS-39).

This photo of "Cape Quonset" shows Quonset carriers and their aircraft, which directly participated in all of the Project Mercury and Project Gemini astronaut launches and recoveries. First was the USS *Lake Champlain*, when Marine Corps HUS-1 from HMR(L)-262 picked up the late Commander Alan B. Shepard, USN, and his Freedom 7 spacecraft on May 5, 1961. All future recoveries would exclusively be performed by Quonset squadrons. (USN/USNI)

SH-3A helos from HS-3 picked up the crew of Gemini 3 March 23, 1965. In addition to providing helos for recovery, S2F, AD and WF fixed-wing aircraft from Quonset ASW Air Groups conducted all of the search, tracking, transfer, and logistics assignments. (NASA)

This view was taken from the cockpit of SH-3A, Gemini 6, on December 16, 1965. The prime recovery ship was the USS Wasp (CVS-18). (NASA)

Again, the *Wasp* was the prime recovery ship. Here, SH-3A helos from HS-11 are ready to pick up the crew of Gemini 9A. (NASA)

HU-2 "Fleet Angels" provided logistics and transfer services aboard all of the Quonset prime recovery ships, initially in the venerable HUP "Hup." (USN/HU-2)

Later, HU-2 employed their new, turbine-powered Kaman HU2K-1 Seasprite. (USN/HC-2)

As naval helicopter performance steadily increased, so did demands made upon HU-2 for more and more shipboard DETs, especially aboard non-aviation ships. To meet this demand, the squadron was split forming a new unit, HU-4 VIS code "HT." HU-4's mission was to supply helicopter utility services to helicopter capable non-aviation ships, mostly cruisers. One of the first DETs got ice breaker duty. Shown here is the USS *Glacier* (AGB-4). (USN)

Some of the first aircraft assigned included Bell HUL-1 HT-25. (USN/HU-4).

By the mid-1960s, the Navy had retired all but one of its axle deck carriers. So long, *Leading Lady*. Quonset's "Champ" would be the last straight deck in the Navy. (USN)

Before it became operational, Quonset's USS *Lake Champlain* carrier qualified the Marines' first turbine-powered heavy lift helicopter, the Sikorsky CH-53A Sea Stallion off Block Island. After successful carquals performed by Marines from HMH-463, MCAS New River, the big helo became operational during November 1966. Within two months, it was on its way to Vietnam. Today, developed as the three-engine, seven-rotor CH-53E, the Super Stallion serves the Corps worldwide as its prime heavy lifter. (Sikorsky)

As the nation's commitment to the Vietnam War deepened, Quonset's Utility Squadron, VC-2, increased its activities. One duty was training fleet pilots in the use of the Sidewinder air-to-air missile in its F-8C (F8U-2) Crusaders JE-23 F-8C. This squadron red shirt is standing on a Sidewinder missile rail. (Hardaker)

VC-2 also increased its commitment to the Cruiser Destroyer Force, Atlantic, Naval Operating Base (NOB) in Newport. This photo was taken at Coddington Cove, NOB Newport, in October 1965. (Naval War College)

Until the Summer of 1967, Quonset was the East Coast head for all A-4 Skyhawk light attack and A-6 Intruder medium attack bombers. These two aircraft were responsible for most of the ordinance dropped on the enemy in Vietnam by the Navy and the Marine Corps. Prop ADs in the attack role were phased out at this time due to SA-2 SAM missile threat. It was at this moment that all jet O&R work went south to Virginia and Florida. (USN/Curry)

By December 1967, Quonset O&R had completed *1,975* A4D Douglas Skyhawk attack jets, which were widely used in Vietnam. (USN Hannan)

A year later, Quonset overhaul lines were all piston engined and prop driven. Here, S2F/S-2 WF-2/E-1B lines are visible. These were very low attrition non-combat active types. The only aircraft that Quonset now produced that went into harms way was prop AD Skyraider, a 20-year-old design in 1965. (USN/Browning)

Quonset had been overhauling, modifying, and rebuilding ADs for the Navy and Marine Corps since 1948. Now, the highly skilled hearts and minds of Quonset's O&R were building them for the USAF and VNAF (South Vietnam). A happy crowd stands in front of the 3,897th AD produced at Quonset. This was more than had been built by the manufacturer at El Segundo! Through the tough years with the fleet, many ADs came back to Mother Quonset again and again, thus producing the high numbers. (Bluin)

Throughout the late 1960s, Quonset continued to produce ADs for the Fleet, such as this AD-5W GE-38, VAW-12. (USN)

After Quonset overhaul, AD-5Ws fly back to the Fleet with VAW-33. The last operational combat flight by the Navy in ADs was made by this squadron in an ECM EA-1F (AD-5Q) in 1971. (USN)

USN AD-6 (A-lH) is on the line for complete overhaul. (USN)

This factory-fresh AD-6 is ready for a test flight. (USN)

By the late 1960s, though, most AD production was going to the orient. Here is a "brand new" sand and spinach A-lH Sandy. (Barthelmes)

This is the A-lE of the USAF 4407th Combat Crew Training Squadron, First Special Operations Wing. They were the famous Air Commandos.

This view shows a USAF Air Commando A-1H Sandy over Florida. (USAF)

This USAF A-1E is fully bombed up with a load of hurt for the Viet Cong. (USAF/Curry)

This photo shows a brace of USAF A-1Hs over the Mekong River, Republic of Vietnam. (USAF)

This is a brace of USAF A-1Es over Yard Country, Vietnam. (USAF)

A doomsday load of nape and other anti-personnel weapons hang from an A-1E Skyraider's bomb racks. (USAF).

Many ADs came back to Quonset via the old USS *Core*, (AKV-43), an aircraft ferry. During World War II, as an Escort carrier (CVE-13), the *Core* frequently operated from Quonset. Her Composite Squadrons, trained and outfitted at Quonset, killed *six* U-boats (see Volume I). (USN/NHC)

The NAS Quonset Point Field Team went to Vietnam. Civilian tech reps from Quonset's O&R worked tirelessly with naval and military personnel on aircraft, equipment, and engines unique to their skills. (Author)

These USMC J-65 jet engines appear here in Vietnam. Back at Quonset, O&R's Engine Shop continued production on these engines for the Navy and Marine Corps A-4 attack aircraft right to the end. (USMC)

O&R and other Quonset commands gave full support to USAF Warning Star operations. The Navy was project head going back to June of 1948 on the original conversion of a Lockheed 749A Constellation commercial airliner to PO-1W (buno 124437) flying radar platform and CIC that developed into the highly successful USN WV-2 Willy Victor and USAF RC/EC-121 line. Quonset support included parts pipeline plus work on APS-20E radar and R-3350, both common in the Navy. Shown here is USAF EC-121H serno 55-129 of the 551st AEW&C Wing, Otis AFB. (USAF/Curry)

It was the old AD though, which fought in three wars, two hot and one cold, that was the consistent bread winner for Quonset O&R for nearly a quarter of a century.

The Second Battle of the North Atlantic, the cat-and-mouse, deadly serious Cold War game between Russia's nuclear submarine armada and the United States Navy's Anti-Submarine Force at Quonset, Commander Quonset ASW, continued without missing a beat. (USN)

Seven

DENOUEMENT

This is the VS-32 S-2E Tracker sub-killing arsenal.

The Anti-Submarine Capitol of the World was located at NAS Quonset Point, Rhode Island. The Department of Defense base loading policies made this seem true in the early 1970s. HS-1 arrived at its new home port July 6, 1970.

In this photo, an HS-1 Transducer is coming down. All of the Navy's East Coast Carrier ASW Squadrons that had not already transferred to Rhode Island began flowing in to Quonset at this time. (USN)

This is the USS *Intrepid*'s HS-3 "Trident" SH-3 holding station. (USN)

Here, an HS-5 SH-3 passes gear to a Newport destroyer. (USN)

This is the HS-7 SH-3D of CVW-3 aboard the USS *Saratoga* (CVA-60) working out the "CV" concept by passing mail to the USS *Pickerel* (SS-524). Note the PUFFs on this SSK Guppy type. (USN)

Born and bred at the great naval air station, Quonset's own HS-9 is seen here with the HSS-2 on the Seaplane Side. (USN)

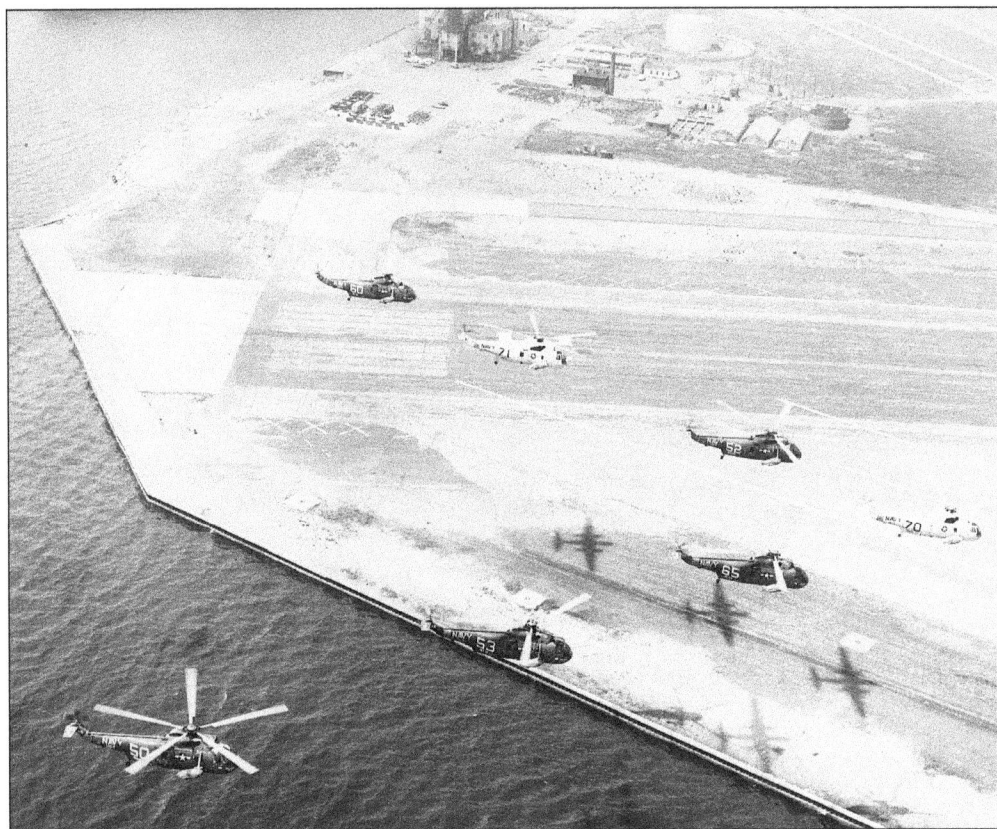

This photo shows the HS-11 SH-3As in both paint schemes on a fly-in from carrier to Quonset after deployment. (USN)

Established at Quonset, Reserve Squadron HS-74 SH-3 is seen here after a remarkable emergency landing on a tiny LAMPs deck aboard a Newport-based ocean Escort. (USN)

The last aircraft turned out by Quonset's NARF (O&R was renamed Naval Air Rework Facility) were Stoofs. Yes, Virginia, the Marine Corps had a few too. MCAS New River US-2B buno 136395 was flown by Marines on proficiency flights as well as utility services. (USMC)

The SH-3G ended the helo line at Quonset's NARF (Naval Air Rework Facility). In this photo from March 1972, a HC-2 SH-3G is making a mail drop to a destroyer in the Gulf of Tonkin. (USN)

Quonset's NARF and Sikorsky worked together in the development of the Navy's first fully functional, operational mine sweeping helicopter, the RH-3A. Note the sweep tow gear under "NAVY." After development, Quonset fabricated installation kits to modify SH-3As to RH-3A standard. (USN)

Quonset, Sikorsky, Navy, and Marine Corps work all came together when, for the first time in the history of mine warfare, helicopters were used to clear mines laid against an enemy. Operation ENDSWEEP was performed by HM-12 and elements of Marine Corps HMH CH-53 Squadrons. Work began on February 27, 1973. This photo shows the giant RH-53D DH-12 of HM-12 lifting sweep gear. (Sikorsky)

The last ASW operations for Quonset Point helped the Navy develop the "CV" concept, in which all carrier-type aircraft would work together from one ship. There would be no more ASW CVS Support Carriers. Quonset's S-2Gs and SH-3Gs proved the theory, and, in this way, may have written their own death warrant. Here, the VS-31 Topcat S-2G moves up to port cat on the *Intrepid*. (USN)

This was the last of its kind. S-2G had many of the internal ASW systems that were being incorporated into its replacement, the VSX S-3A. (USN)

This is an artist's concept of Lockheed's S-3A VSX proposal over a superimposed ASW Task Group. It was believed that Quonset was to be the Overhaul Head for this new turbofan sub hunter.

Unfortunately, NAS Quonset Point was closed in 1974 and all ASW assets were transferred to naval air stations in Florida. (USN)

Near the end, VS-31 is on parade with their S-2G Trackers. The *Essex* looms in the distance at the Carrier Pier. (USN)

VS-34 is shown here on parade with their S-2Es.

The last official landing at Quonset was made with the air station's unique two-tail Cod, buno 138792, on April 4, 1974. (USN/PC)

The "792" two-tail Cod was once the aerodynamic prototype for the WF-2, the grand pappy of all "Fudds" on the QAM wish list. (USN/PC)

This photo depicts Quonset as a vital industrial naval air station. (USN)

This is Quonset in the era of Electric Boat and the Rhode Island Department of Economic Development. (RIDED)

126

No more stoofs . . .　　　(USN)

No more carriers . . .　　　(USN)

All gone . . . but not forgotten. (USN)

9 781531 600280